A Secret for successful baking

Successful baking is another way of keeping a family happy. For who isn't filled with the joy of living when tempted by the penetrating aroma of Gingerbread, rich and spicy ... or a piece of luscious velvety Chocolate Cake, full of flavor? What adds more zest to a meal than a surprise plate of hot breads ... fragrant Cinnamon Buns, maybe Lemon Clover Rolls, delicate Soda Biscuits or Old Fashioned Corn Bread?

The secret for making these successfully is as "old as the hills" but as new as the morrow. Baking soda! Yes, grandmother used it in her prized recipes and the modern homemaker finds it making her baking day a success.

Arm & Hammer Brand and Cow Brand Baking Soda are refined bicarbonate of soda whose standard of purity is that set up by the United States Pharmacopoeia. For over 90 years this mild, healthful, alkaline substance has been creating baking history. All these years homemakers have depended on baking soda to make their baked products deliciously moist and delicately light and tender.

"How," asks the inexperienced homemaker, "does baking soda make cakes, cookies and quick breads light and tender every time?"

Baking soda has stored in it a tremendous quantity of carbon dioxide gas, the same gas found in soda water and ginger ale. This is released when it comes in contact with any acid material such as the many mild acids naturally found in cooking ingredients.

Among those ingredients are chocolate, cocoa, brown sugar, tomato juice, sour milk, buttermilk, apple sauce, spices, cottage cheese, molasses, vinegar, citrus fruit juices and many more. These acid ingredients are familiar to everyone. One or more of them, you will notice, is used almost every time you bake.

The baking soda gently but surely reacts with these natural acids, freeing millions of tiny carbon dioxide bubbles which are held enmeshed in the batters and doughs. As this gas expands during the baking, the product becomes light and tender. Thus it is that baking soda uses nature's own unrivaled acids to leaven and lighten baked products.

Success Assured

Leavening nature's way is surprisingly easy. The acid content of citrus fruit juices or vinegar may be used to develop the unsurpassed flavor and texture associated with baking soda products. The following amounts,

    1⅓ tablespoons vinegar (4 teaspoons)
    1½ tablespoons lemon juice (4½ teaspoons)
    ¾ cup orange juice (12 tablespoons)

may be used with ½ teaspoon baking soda. Many of the recipes in this booklet are especially designed for this natural combination of baking soda and acid juices. Sometimes the acid is added last as in the "Lemon Loaf Cake" on page 11, while in the "Lemon Clover Rolls," page 28, it is combined with the liquid, then added to the mixture. In any case, you will be pleased with the results.

IMPORTANT! You don't need natural sour milk or buttermilk to prepare your old time favorite delicacies. It is the acid normally found in these ingredients which reacts with baking soda for leavening. If sour milk or buttermilk with its natural acid is not available, you may provide the necessary acid by using citrus fruit juices or vinegar with sweet milk. It is surprisingly simple to change sweet milk to milk that contains as much acid as natural sour milk or buttermilk when it is at its best for baking.

For example, when vinegar is used to provide this acid, place 1⅓ tablespoons vinegar (white vinegar makes a whiter product) in a standard measuring cup, then fill to the one-cup mark with sweet milk. Mix well. The resulting liquid can be used in place of sour milk or buttermilk in any baking soda recipe. Use 1½ tablespoons lemon juice or ¾ cup orange juice in a similar manner.

In many of these recipes, designed in our Research Test Kitchen, one or more acid ingredient is used to create perfect leavening with baking soda.

Follow these recipes accurately and carefully, then enjoy the finer flavor and even texture produced when baking with baking soda.

How to Bake

FLOUR. Preferably use the kind of flour specified in the recipe. If you substitute cake or pastry flour for all-purpose flour, use 2 additional tablespoonfuls of flour for each cup required; to substitute all-purpose flour for cake or pastry flour, remove 2 tablespoonfuls of flour from each cup.

FATS. Solid fats can be used interchangeably. Melted fats or oils should not be used in recipes specifying creaming of the shortening.

LIQUID. The use of citrus fruit juices, lemon and orange, is the most recent accompaniment with sweet milk and baking soda for leavening. With the health-giving qualities, this new use for fruit juices in baking is widely accepted.

Sweet milk may be used in place of sour milk if clabbered artificially. To sour or clabber sweet milk quickly, place 1½ tablespoonfuls of lemon juice or 1⅓ tablespoonfuls of vinegar (white vinegar makes a whiter product) in a standard measuring cup, then fill to the one-cup mark with sweet milk. Mix well. The resulting liquid will contain as much acid as natural sour milk or buttermilk when it is at its best for baking, and may be used exactly as natural sour milk or buttermilk in any baking soda recipe.

MEASURING. Always use level measurements. Use standard measuring equipment: a ½ pint cup marked in quarters and thirds; a set of standard measuring spoons consisting of a tablespoon, teaspoon, ½ teaspoon and ¼ teaspoon.

MIXING. There is no such thing as "luck" in baking. Success depends on good ingredients correctly combined. Follow the directions carefully as set down in the following recipes.

BAKING. Keep the oven at the temperature specified in the recipe. You have mastered an important part of baking, if you keep your oven under control. Oven regulators and thermometers safeguard baking.

CARE AFTER BAKING. Let cakes stand in pan on cooling rack for 3 to 5 minutes after baking; then turn out on rack and finish cooling before frosting. Cookies should also be cooled on a rack.

ALWAYS SIFT FLOUR

Facts Regarding Plain White Flour

In Arm & Hammer or Cow Brand Baking Soda recipes, certain types of flour are used or specified simply to indicate that such a flour gives the most desirable characteristics to that particular baked product, but it does not mean that another type of flour cannot be substituted, nor that an inferior product will result if a correct substitution is made.

BREAD FLOUR. This is used to a large extent by commercial bakers and generally is made from hard wheats: it contains a high percentage of a protein product known as gluten. The gluten in this flour is hard, capable of taking up and retaining a large quantity of water. This type of flour is admirably adapted for bread making, since the strong gluten gives an excellent skeleton to the loaf. Such a flour is seldom used in the home today, except by those who make large quantities of home-made white bread. Usually, the gluten is present in this flour to the extent of 11 to 12%.

GENERAL PURPOSE OR FAMILY FLOUR. This flour is intended to fill all needs and, consequently, is made by blending flours from soft and hard wheats. It contains a moderate amount of medium hard gluten, and is used in baking hot breads, such as muffins and scones. However, it can be used for pastries as well. When employed in place of pastry or cake flour, two level tablespoonfuls less per cup should be used. General-purpose flours range in gluten content from 10 to 11% and, in this respect, are about half way between bread and true pastry or cake flours.

PASTRY OR CAKE FLOUR. Such flours not only have the lowest gluten content, but a weak soft gluten as well, and are very satisfactory for making all pastries except such items as fruit cakes. These are preferably made with all-purpose flour, to support the fruit and maintain a desirable structure. Pastry flours contain 9 to 10% gluten and are made from various types of soft wheat. Special cake flours belong to the pastry flour class, but are finer in texture. They are slightly lower in gluten content (8 to 9%), and the gluten is even softer. Pastry flour gives baked products a tender thin crust and a delicate crumb. Pastry flour can neither absorb nor retain moisture like bread and all-purpose flours and, therefore, sour milk or buttermilk is splendidly adapted for use with this flour, since both are capable of retaining moisture.

If all-purpose or family flour is specified in a recipe, and only pastry is available, increase the pastry flour slightly (two tablespoonfuls for every cup of family flour specified). When pastry flour is used in biscuit recipes, the dough is rather soft and inclined to be somewhat difficult to roll. Instead of further increasing the pastry flour to stiffen the dough, better results are realized by using the dough for dropped biscuits.

Flour, baking soda and many other similar materials should be stored in a dry cool place, free from odors.

Cakes

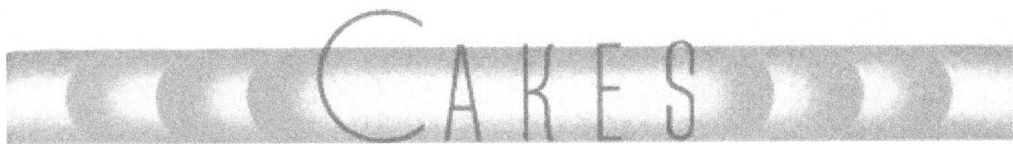

ORANGE LOAF

2 cups pastry flour
½ teaspoon Arm & Hammer or Cow Brand Baking Soda
¼ teaspoon salt
⅓ cup butter, or other shortening
1 cup sugar
2 eggs
Grated rind of 1 orange
¾ cup orange juice, strained

1. Sift, then measure the flour. Sift three times with the baking soda and salt.

2. Cream the butter until light and lemon colored. Add sugar gradually, beating after each addition.

3. Slowly add the eggs which have been beaten until they are almost as stiff as whipped cream.

4. Add the orange rind. Alternately add the dry ingredients and orange juice, beating until smooth after each addition.

5. Turn into a greased paper lined loaf pan. Bake.

6. When cool frost with Coconut Orange Frosting.

Amount: 6×10 inch pan   *Temperature: 350° F.*   *Time: 50 minutes*
<u>See page 8</u>

MARBLE CAKE

2½ cups pastry flour
1 teaspoon Arm & Hammer or Cow Brand Baking Soda
¼ teaspoon salt
½ cup butter, or other shortening
1 cup sugar
2 eggs
2 tablespoons lemon juice
¾ cup sweet milk
½ teaspoon vanilla
1 teaspoon cinnamon
½ teaspoon cloves
¼ teaspoon nutmeg
¼ teaspoon Arm & Hammer or Cow Brand Baking Soda
1 tablespoon molasses

1. Sift, then measure the flour. Sift three times with the 1 teaspoon baking soda and salt.

2. Cream the butter until light and lemon colored. Add sugar gradually, beating after each addition.

3. Slowly add the eggs which have been beaten until they are almost as stiff as whipped cream.

4. Combine the lemon juice and milk. Alternately add the dry ingredients and the liquid, a small amount at a time, beating until smooth after each addition.

5. Divide batter in two equal parts.

6. To part one, add the vanilla.

7. To the other, add the well mixed ¼ teaspoon baking soda and spices, then the molasses. Blend well.

8. Place batter in greased loaf pan by spoonfuls, alternating the light and dark batters, thus giving a marbled effect. Bake.

9. Frost with Butter Frosting.

   Amount: 9×5 inch pan   Temperature: 350° F.   Time: 45-50 minutes
   <u>See page 8</u>

DATE NUT LAYER CAKE

2⅓ cups all-purpose flour
¾ teaspoon Arm & Hammer or Cow Brand Baking Soda
½ teaspoon salt
½ cup butter, or other shortening
1 cup sugar
2 eggs
1 cup buttermilk
1 cup dates, very finely cut
1 cup nutmeats, coarsely chopped

1. Sift, then measure the flour. Sift three times with baking soda and salt. All-purpose flour is used to prevent settling of dates to the bottom of the cake.

2. Cream the butter until light and lemon colored. Add sugar gradually, beating after each addition.

3. Slowly add the eggs which have been beaten until they are almost as stiff as whipped cream.

4. Alternately add the dry ingredients and the liquid, beating until smooth after each addition.

5. Quickly fold in the dates and nuts which have been floured with 1 tablespoon of the dry ingredients.

6. Turn into greased layer cake pans. Bake.

7. Frost with Maple Cream Frosting.

Amount: 2—9 inch pans   Temperature: 350° F.   Time: 30-35 minutes

SOUR MILK CHOCOLATE CAKE

2 cups pastry flour
1 teaspoon Arm & Hammer or Cow Brand Baking Soda
¼ teaspoon salt
½ cup butter, or other shortening
1 cup sugar
2 eggs
2 squares (2 ounces) unsweetened chocolate
1 cup sour milk
1 teaspoon vanilla

1. Sift, then measure flour. Sift three times with baking soda and salt.

2. Cream the butter until light and lemon colored. Add sugar gradually, beating after each addition.

3. Slowly add the eggs which have been beaten until they are almost as stiff as whipped cream.

4. Gradually add the chocolate which has been melted and cooled.

5. Stir the vanilla into the milk. Alternately add the dry ingredients and the liquid, a small amount at a time, beating until smooth after each addition.

6. Turn into a greased loaf pan. Bake.

7. Frost with Soft Chocolate Icing.

Amount: 8×8 inch pan   *Temperature: 325° F.*   *Time: 60 minutes*

DESSERT GINGERBREAD

1½ cups all-purpose flour
1 teaspoon Arm & Hammer or Cow Brand Baking Soda
¼ teaspoon salt
1 teaspoon ginger
⅓ cup shortening
½ cup sugar
1 egg
½ cup molasses
¾ cup boiling water

1. Sift, then measure the flour. Sift three times with the baking soda, salt and ginger.

2. Cream the shortening until it is light and fluffy. Add the sugar gradually, beating after each addition.

3. Next, add the unbeaten egg, beating briskly.

4. Add the molasses. Then add the dry ingredients, beating until smooth. Stir in boiling water.

5. Turn into greased loaf pan. Bake.

   Amount: 8×8 inch pan   *Temperature: 350° F.*   *Time: 30-40 minutes*
   <u>See page 8</u>

LEMON LOAF CAKE

2 cups pastry flour
½ teaspoon Arm & Hammer or Cow Brand Baking Soda
¼ teaspoon salt

½ cup butter, or other shortening
1 cup sugar
2 eggs
½ cup sweet milk
1½ tablespoons lemon juice

1. Sift, then measure flour. Sift three times with baking soda and salt.

2. Cream the butter until light and lemon colored. Add sugar gradually.

3. Slowly add the eggs which have been beaten until they are almost as stiff as whipped cream.

4. Alternately add the dry ingredients and the liquid, beating until smooth after each addition. Add lemon juice, blending in well.

5. Turn into greased loaf pan. Bake.

6. Cover with Lemon Filling and top with ½ recipe of Fluffy Frosting.

Amount: 8×8 inch pan   Temperature 350° F.   Time: 45 minutes
<u>See page 17</u>

THANKSGIVING STEAMED PUDDING

3 cups all-purpose flour
1 teaspoon Arm & Hammer or Cow Brand Baking Soda
1½ teaspoons salt
½ teaspoon cloves
½ teaspoon mace
½ teaspoon allspice
½ teaspoon cinnamon
1 cup suet, finely ground
1 cup molasses
1 cup sweet milk
1½ cups seedless raisins, chopped

1. Sift, then measure the flour. Sift three times with the baking soda, salt and spices.

2. Combine suet, molasses and milk.

3. To the suet mixture, add the dry ingredients, beating until smooth. Add raisins.

4. Turn into a well greased pan or mold. Cover. Steam 3 hours.

5. Serve with Hard Sauce or Foamy Sauce.

Amount:12servings

DARK FRUIT CAKE

5 cups all-purpose flour
1 teaspoon Arm & Hammer or Cow Brand Baking Soda
½ teaspoon salt
½ teaspoon cloves
½ teaspoon cinnamon
½ teaspoon mace
1 pound butter, or other shortening
1 pound sifted brown sugar
8 eggs
½ pound each candied cherries, citron, orange and lemon peel, finely sliced
1 pound almonds, blanched and shredded
1 pound seedless raisins
1 pound currants
½ cup water
1 cup honey
½ cup molasses

1. Sift, then measure the flour. Sift three times with baking soda, salt and spices.

2. Cream the butter until light and lemon colored. Add sugar gradually, beating after each addition.

3. Slowly add the eggs which have been beaten until they are almost as stiff as whipped cream.

4. Add the fruits and nuts, then add water, honey and molasses.

5. Add dry ingredients, beating until smooth after each addition.

6. Turn into 2 paper-lined tube pans. Bake.

Amount: 10 pounds   Temperature: 250° F.   Time: 3½ hours

BAKED PRUNE PUDDING

1½ cups all-purpose flour
½ teaspoon Arm & Hammer or Cow Brand Baking Soda
½ teaspoon salt
½ teaspoon cinnamon
¼ cup butter, or other shortening
¾ cup sugar
1 egg
½ cup juice from prunes
1 cup stewed prunes, drained and finely chopped
½ cup nutmeats, coarsely cut

1. Sift, then measure flour. Sift three times with baking soda, salt and cinnamon.

2. Cream the butter until it is light and lemon colored. Add sugar gradually, beating after each addition.

3. Briskly stir in the well beaten egg.

4. Alternately add the dry ingredients and prune juice, a small amount at a time, beating until smooth after each addition.

5. Last, carefully stir in the prunes and nutmeats.

6. Turn into a greased tube pan. Bake.

7. Serve with whipped cream.

Amount: 2 qt. tube pan   Temperature: 375° F.   Time: 1 hour

FAVORITE SPICE CAKE

2½ cups pastry flour
1 teaspoon Arm & Hammer or Cow Brand Baking Soda
¼ teaspoon salt
2 teaspoons cinnamon
½ teaspoon cloves
¼ teaspoon nutmeg
½ cup butter, or other shortening
1 cup sifted brown sugar, firmly packed
2 eggs
¾ cup sweet milk
2 tablespoons vinegar

1. Sift, then measure flour. Sift again with baking soda, salt and spices.

2. Cream butter until light and lemon colored. Add sugar gradually, beating after each addition.

3. Slowly add the eggs which have been beaten until they are almost as thick as whipped cream.

4. Combine vinegar and milk. Alternately add the dry and the liquid ingredients, beating until smooth after each addition.

5. Turn into a greased cake pan. Bake in a moderate oven.

6. Frost with Butter Frosting.

Amount: 8×8 inch pan *Temperature: 350° F.* *Time: 40-45 minutes*

RED DEVIL'S CAKE

2 cups pastry flour
1¼ teaspoons Arm & Hammer Cow Brand Baking Soda
¼ teaspoon salt
½ cup butter, or other shortening
1 cup sugar
2 eggs
2 squares (2 ounces) unsweetened chocolate
1 teaspoon vanilla
¾ cup sour milk or buttermilk
⅓ cup boiling water

1. Sift, then measure the flour. Sift three times with the baking soda and salt.

2. Cream the butter until light and lemon colored. Add sugar gradually, beating after each addition until light and fluffy.

3. Slowly add the eggs which have been beaten until they are almost as stiff as whipped cream. Gradually add the chocolate which has been melted and cooled.

4. Stir the vanilla into the milk. Alternately add the dry ingredients and the milk, beating until smooth after each addition. Add the boiling water and beat in well.

5. Turn into a greased cake pan. Bake.

6. Frost with Quick Butterscotch Icing. Let cake stand two hours before cutting to allow the red color to develop.

Amount: 2—8 inch layers *Temperature: 350° F.* *Time: 25-30 minutes*

See page 17

HONEY DIAMONDS

2 cups pastry flour
½ teaspoon Arm & Hammer or Cow Brand Baking Soda
¼ teaspoon salt
½ teaspoon cinnamon
¼ cup butter, or other shortening
1 cup sifted brown sugar, firmly packed
⅓ cup honey
2 eggs
½ cup sweet milk
Nutmeats

1. Sift, then measure the flour. Sift three times with the baking soda, salt and cinnamon.

2. Cream the butter until light and lemon colored. Add sugar gradually, beating after each addition.

3. Combine honey and eggs which have been beaten until they are almost as stiff as whipped cream. Add to the butter-sugar mixture. Blend well.

4. Alternately add the dry ingredients and milk, beating after each addition.

5. Turn into a greased shallow cake pan. Bake.

6. Frost with Butter Icing. Garnish with nutmeats. Cut in diamond shaped pieces.

Amount: 9×9 inch pan   Temperature: 350° F.   Time: 45-50 minutes
<u>See page 8</u>

FRUIT CUP CAKES

2 cups pastry flour
1 teaspoon Arm & Hammer or Cow Brand Baking Soda

½ teaspoon salt
1 teaspoon cinnamon
½ teaspoon allspice
½ cup butter, or other shortening
1 cup sifted brown sugar, firmly packed
2 eggs
1⅓ tablespoons vinegar
⅔ cup sweet milk
1 cup dates, finely cut
1 cup nutmeats, coarsely cut
½ cup citron, sliced

1. Sift, then measure the flour. Sift three times with baking soda, salt and spices.

2. Cream the butter until light and lemon colored. Add sugar gradually, beating after each addition.

3. Slowly add the eggs which have been beaten until they are almost as thick as whipped cream.

4. Combine vinegar and milk. Alternately add the dry ingredients and the liquid, a small amount at a time, beating until smooth after each addition.

5. Lastly add fruit and nuts.

6. Fill greased muffin tins ⅔ full.

Amount: 3 dozen small cakes   Temperature: 375° F.   Time: 20-25 minutes
<u>See page 17</u>

APPLE SAUCE CAKE

2 cups all-purpose flour
1 teaspoon Arm & Hammer or Cow Brand Baking Soda

¼ teaspoon salt
¼ teaspoon cloves
½ teaspoon nutmeg
1 teaspoon cinnamon
½ cup butter, or other shortening
1 cup sugar
1 egg
1 cup raisins, chopped
1 cup nutmeats, coarsely broken
1 cup thick apple sauce

1. Sift, then measure the flour. Sift three times with the baking soda, salt and spice.

2. Cream the butter well. Gradually add sugar, beating after each addition.

3. Add the egg, beating well, then the raisins and nuts.

4. Alternately add the dry ingredients and apple sauce, beating until smooth after each addition.

5. Turn into a greased loaf pan. Bake.

Amount: 9×9 inch pan   Temperature: 350° F.   Time: 1 hour 15 minutes

CHOCOLATE NUT CAKE

1⅓ cups pastry flour
¾ teaspoon Arm & Hammer or Cow Brand Baking Soda
½ teaspoon salt
⅓ cup butter, or other shortening
¾ cup sugar
1 egg
½ cup nutmeats, coarsely cut
2 ounces (2 squares) unsweetened chocolate
¾ cup sour milk or buttermilk

1 teaspoon vanilla

1. Sift, then measure flour. Sift again with the baking soda and salt.

2. Cream the butter until light and lemon colored. Add the sugar gradually, beating after each addition.

3. Slowly add the egg which has been beaten until it is almost as stiff as whipped cream.

4. Add the nutmeats, then the chocolate which has been melted and cooled.

5. Combine the vanilla and sour milk. Alternately add the dry and liquid ingredients, beating until smooth after each addition.

6. Turn into greased pan and bake in moderate oven.

Amount: 8×8 inch pan or a tube pan　　　*Temperature: 350° F.*
　　　Time: 40-45 minutes　See page 17

Frostings

ORANGE COCONUT FROSTING

3 tablespoons butter
2 cups confectioners sugar
¼ cup orange juice
¾ cup grated coconut

1. Cream butter until very soft.

2. Add sugar gradually, thinning with orange juice to spreading consistency. Beat until smooth.

3. Beat coconut into frosting.

Amount: 1½ cups   See page 8

FOAMY SAUCE

½ cup butter
1 cup confectioners sugar
2 egg yolks
¼ cup brandy
2 egg whites

1. Cream butter until light and lemon colored.

2. Gradually add sugar, beating until light and fluffy.

3. Add egg yolks, one at a time, beating until well blended.

4. Add brandy. Place in upper part of double boiler over simmering water and cook until thickened, stirring constantly.

5. Pour slowly over egg whites which have been stiffly beaten. Blend gently but thoroughly. Serve immediately.

Amount:2cups

MAPLE CREAM FROSTING

½ cup maple syrup
1 pound confectioners sugar
¼ cup butter, melted
¼ cup milk
Dash of salt

1. Heat maple syrup to boiling and cook 3 minutes.

2. Combine sugar, butter, milk and salt.

3. Add syrup and beat until light and thick.

4. This makes sufficient frosting to generously cover tops of two 9-inch layers.

BUTTER FROSTING

4 tablespoons butter
2 cups confectioners sugar

2 tablespoons milk
1 teaspoon vanilla

1. Cream butter until very soft.

2. Add sugar gradually, thinning with milk until it is of spreading consistency.

3. Add vanilla. Beat until smooth.

Amount:1cup   See page 8

QUICK BUTTERSCOTCH FROSTING

2 tablespoons granulated sugar
¼ cup boiling water
2½ cups confectioners sugar
¼ cup milk
2 tablespoons butter

1. Make a caramel syrup of the granulated sugar by heating it slowly over a flame until it melts and becomes straw colored. Remove from fire. Add boiling water carefully as it spatters. Stir until sugar is dissolved.

2. Cream butter until soft. Add ½ cup of confectioners sugar. Then add sugar syrup, beating well. Add remaining confectioners sugar gradually, thinning with milk to a spreading consistency.

FLUFFY FROSTING

1 cup sugar
2 egg whites
4 tablespoons cold water
¼ teaspoon cream of tartar
Dash of salt
½ teaspoon vanilla

1. Combine sugar, unbeaten egg whites, water, cream of tartar and salt in upper part of double boiler.

2. Place over boiling water and beat constantly with rotary type beater until frosting will stand in peaks, or about 7 minutes. Add vanilla last.

Amount: 3 cups   See page 17

SOFT CHOCOLATE FROSTING

1 cup confectioners sugar
1 egg
Dash of salt
2 squares (2 ounces) unsweetened chocolate
½ teaspoon vanilla

1. Gradually add sugar to the slightly beaten egg. Beat until smooth and light.

2. Add salt and melted chocolate, blending well. Add vanilla. Cool before spreading.

3. This makes sufficient to cover tops and sides of an 8 × 8 inch loaf cake.

LEMON FILLING

Juice and grated rind of 1 lemon
½ cup sugar
¾ cup water
2½ tablespoons cornstarch
2 tablespoons water
1 egg yolk

1. Combine lemon juice, rind, sugar and ¾ cup water. Slowly bring this mixture to boiling point.

2. Make a smooth paste of cornstarch and the 2 tablespoons of water. Add slowly to syrup, stirring constantly. Cook until mixture is thick and clear, or about 5 minutes. Remove from heat.

3. Add small amount to slightly beaten egg yolk. Beat vigorously. Return to remaining mixture and blend well. Cool.

Amount: 1½ cups   See page 17

Cookies

COCONUT ICEBOX COOKIES

4 cups all-purpose flour
1 teaspoon Arm & Hammer or Cow Brand Baking Soda
1 teaspoon salt
1 teaspoon cinnamon
1 cup melted butter, or other shortening
1 cup granulated sugar
½ cup sifted brown sugar, firmly packed
2 eggs
2 cups shredded coconut
½ cup sweet milk

1. Sift, then measure the flour. Sift again with the baking soda, salt and cinnamon.

2. Combine melted shortening, granulated sugar, brown sugar, well beaten eggs, coconut and milk. Reserve part of coconut for garnish if desired.

3. To this mixture blend in the dry ingredients.

4. Form into two rolls 6 inches long. Wrap in wax paper. Place in refrigerator until thoroughly chilled or as needed.

5. Cut ¼ inch slices from roll as required. Bake in hot oven.

Amount: 4 dozen cookies   Temperature: 425° F.   Time: 5-8 minutes
<u>See page 20</u>

SOFT MOLASSES COOKIES

4½ cups all-purpose flour
2 teaspoons Arm & Hammer or Cow Brand Baking Soda
3 teaspoons ginger
1 teaspoon salt
1 cup butter, or other shortening
1 cup sifted brown sugar, firmly packed
2 eggs
¾ cup molasses
¾ cup sour milk
Granulated sugar

1. Sift, then measure the flour. Sift again with the baking soda, ginger and salt.

2. Cream shortening, add sugar gradually and beat until light and fluffy.

3. Blend in the well beaten eggs. Then add molasses and continue beating.

4. Alternately add the dry ingredients with the milk, beating until smooth after each addition.

5. Chill dough in refrigerator several hours.

6. Turn onto floured board. Roll to ¼-inch thickness and cut with scalloped cooky cutter, or form a roll of the dough and cut slices ¼ inch thick. Sprinkle with granulated sugar.

7. Place on greased baking sheet. Bake in a hot oven.

Amount: 3 dozen, 3-inch cookies   Temperature: 400° F.   Time: 12 minutes

FRUIT COOKIES

    3½ cups all-purpose flour
    1 teaspoon Arm & Hammer or Cow Brand Baking Soda
    ½ teaspoon salt
    1 teaspoon cinnamon
    1 teaspoon nutmeg
    ¾ cup butter
    1 cup sugar
    2 eggs
    ¾ cup molasses
    1 cup raisins
    1 cup nutmeats, coarsely cut

1. Sift, then measure the flour. Sift three times with the baking soda, salt and spices.

2. Cream the butter until light and lemon colored. Add sugar gradually.

3. Slowly add the well beaten eggs, then the molasses, blending thoroughly.

4. Add the dry ingredients, beating until smooth.

5. Last, stir in the raisins and nuts.

6. Chill in refrigerator until firm enough to handle.

7. Turn onto a lightly floured board. Roll as thin as possible without causing dough to break. Cut with large size, floured cutter.

8. Bake on an ungreased baking sheet in a hot oven.

Amount: 3½ dozen cookies   Temperature: 425° F.   Time: 8-10 minutes

FROSTED CHOCOLATE DROPS

1¾ cups all-purpose flour
½ teaspoon Arm & Hammer or Cow Brand Baking Soda
½ teaspoon salt
½ cup butter, or other shortening
¾ cup sugar
1 egg
2 squares (2 ounces) unsweetened chocolate
1 teaspoon vanilla
½ cup sweet milk
½ cup nutmeats, coarsely cut

1. Sift, then measure the flour. Sift three times with the baking soda and salt.

2. Cream the butter until light and lemon colored. Add sugar gradually, beating after each addition.

3. Slowly add the well beaten egg, then the chocolate which has been melted and cooled.

4. Stir vanilla into the milk. Alternately add dry ingredients and liquid, beating until smooth after each addition. Stir in nutmeats.

5. Drop by spoonfuls on ungreased baking sheet. Bake in hot oven.

6. When cool, frost with Soft Chocolate Frosting.

Amount: 3 dozen cookies   Temperature: 425° F.   Time: 8-10 minutes
See page 20

OLD FASHIONED MOLASSES COOKIES

8 cups all-purpose flour
4 teaspoons Arm & Hammer or Cow Brand Baking Soda
¼ teaspoon salt
1 tablespoon ginger

1 teaspoon cinnamon
3 cups molasses
1 cup lard, melted
½ cup butter, melted
10 tablespoons boiling water
Granulated sugar

1. Sift, then measure the flour. Sift three times with the baking soda, salt and spices.

2. Combine the molasses, melted shortening and boiling water.

3. To these liquid ingredients, add 4 cups of dry ingredients and blend well.

4. Add remaining 4 cups of dry ingredients gradually, beating well after each addition.

5. Let stand in a cool place about 1 hour.

6. Turn onto a lightly floured board. Roll ¼ inch thick. Cut with large, floured cooky cutter. Sprinkle with granulated sugar. Bake in hot oven.

Amount: 5 dozen cookies   Temperature: 425° F.   Time: 15 minutes

CRISP WHITE SUGAR COOKIES

4 cups all-purpose flour
1 teaspoon Arm & Hammer or Cow Brand Baking Soda
½ teaspoon salt
1½ cups sugar
1½ cups butter, or other shortening
½ cup sour milk or buttermilk
2 eggs
1 teaspoon vanilla

1. Sift, then measure the flour. Sift again with the baking soda, salt and sugar.

2. Cut the shortening into the dry ingredients until it is as fine as corn meal.

3. Combine milk, slightly beaten eggs and vanilla.

4. Add the dry ingredients to the liquid ingredients, beating until smooth.

5. Cover dough closely with wax paper and chill in refrigerator overnight or several hours.

6. Then turn dough on a lightly floured board and roll thin. Cut with a floured cooky cutter. Garnish. Keep dough cold as it becomes sticky and hard to handle when warm.

7. Bake on ungreased baking sheet in a hot oven.

8. Remove to cooling rack. They will crisp as they cool.

Amount: 4 dozen large cookies   Temperature: 425° F.   Time: 8-10 minutes
See page 20

DOUGHNUTS

4 cups all-purpose flour
1 teaspoon Arm & Hammer or Cow Brand Baking Soda
1 teaspoon salt
¼ teaspoon cinnamon
½ teaspoon nutmeg
2 eggs
2 tablespoons shortening, melted
1 cup sugar
1 cup sour milk

1. Sift, then measure the flour. Sift three times with the baking soda, salt and spices.

2. Beat eggs slightly. Combine beaten eggs, shortening, sugar and sour milk.

3. Add flour mixture, stirring as little as possible. Chill.

4. Turn onto floured board. Roll or pat ⅓ inch thick. Cut with floured doughnut cutter.

5. The fat, when ready for frying doughnuts, should be 360°-375° F., or it should brown a cube of bread in 60 seconds.

6. Carefully drop each doughnut into the fat to prevent splashing. Fry not more than 4 or 5 doughnuts at one time or fat will be cooled too quickly. Fry to a delicate brown, turning doughnuts once.

7. Drain on unglazed paper and sprinkle with sugar.

Amount: 2½ dozen   See page 20

RAISIN ROCKS

2 cups all-purpose flour
1 teaspoon Arm & Hammer or Cow Brand Baking Soda
1 teaspoon salt
½ teaspoon cloves
1 teaspoon cinnamon
½ teaspoon nutmeg
½ cup butter, or other shortening
½ cup sugar
1 egg
½ cup sour milk
½ cup molasses
1 cup seedless raisins or currants
½ cup nutmeats, coarsely chopped

1. Sift, then measure flour. Sift three times with baking soda, salt and spices.

2. Cream the butter until light and lemon colored. Add sugar gradually, beating after each addition.

3. Add the unbeaten egg, blending well.

4. Combine milk and molasses. Alternately add dry ingredients and the liquid, beating until smooth after each addition.

5. Add raisins and nuts. Drop by spoonfuls on ungreased baking sheet. Bake in hot oven.

Amount: 3 dozen Rocks   Temperature: 400° F.   Time: 10-12 minutes
See page 20

BISCUITS

SODA BISCUITS

2 cups all-purpose flour
½ teaspoon Arm & Hammer or Cow Brand Baking Soda
½ teaspoon salt
4 tablespoons shortening
¾ cup sour milk or buttermilk (about)

1. Sift, then measure flour. Sift again with the baking soda and salt.

2. Using the finger tips or a pastry blender, rub or cut shortening into the dry ingredients until the mixture resembles coarse corn meal.

3. To sour ¾ cup sweet milk artificially and quickly, place 1 tablespoon lemon juice or vinegar (preferably white vinegar as it makes a whiter biscuit) in a measuring cup, fill ¾ full with sweet milk and mix well.

4. Make a well in the center of the mixture and turn in the sour milk or buttermilk all at once, reserving about 1 tablespoon of the liquid as it may not be required.

5. Then stir to make a soft dough as quickly as possible, using a fork. Add remainder of liquid if necessary.

6. As soon as the flour has been gathered together, turn the dough onto a floured board. The dough should be stiff but soft to the touch and not

sticky.

7. Knead the dough lightly for about 30 seconds, using the palm of the hand and finger tips.

8. Then pat or roll to a thickness of about ½ inch. Cut with floured biscuit cutter.

9. Place biscuits on ungreased baking sheet. Bake in hot oven.

Amount: 12—2 inch biscuits   Temperature: 475° F.   Time: 12-15 minutes   See page 24

CHEESE TEA BISCUITS

1½ cups all-purpose flour
½ teaspoon Arm & Hammer or Cow Brand Baking Soda
½ teaspoon salt
4 tablespoons shortening
1 cup grated cheese
¾ cup sour milk or buttermilk

1. Sift, then measure flour. Sift again with the baking soda and salt.

2. Cut or rub in shortening until it is as fine as coarse corn meal. Add cheese to this mixture.

3. Add sour milk, stirring quickly to form a soft dough.

4. Drop by teaspoonfuls onto a baking sheet. Bake in hot oven.

Amount: 18 small biscuits   Temperature: 475° F.   Time: 12 minutes

COFFEE CAKE

2½ cups all-purpose flour
½ teaspoon salt
1 cup sifted brown sugar, firmly packed
½ cup butter, or other shortening
1 teaspoon Arm & Hammer or Cow Brand Baking Soda
1 teaspoon cinnamon
1 egg
¾ cup sour milk or buttermilk

1. Sift, then measure flour. Sift again with salt. Add brown sugar and mix well.

2. Cut or rub in shortening until it resembles coarse crumbs. Reserve ¾ cup of crumbs for topping.

3. To remainder, add baking soda and cinnamon. Mix well.

4. Combine well beaten egg and sour milk. Then add liquid to dry ingredients. Stir only until blended.

5. Turn into a greased pan. Sprinkle with the ¾ cup crumbs and additional cinnamon. Bake in hot oven. Serve hot.

Amount: 8 × 8 inch pan   Temperature: 400° F.   Time: 30 minutes

CINNAMON BUNS

2 cups all-purpose flour
½ teaspoon Arm & Hammer or Cow Brand Baking Soda
½ teaspoon salt
1 tablespoon sugar
4 tablespoons shortening
¾ cup sour milk or buttermilk (about)
Butter
¼ cup sugar
½ teaspoon cinnamon

1. Sift, then measure flour. Sift again with the baking soda, salt and sugar.

2. Cut or rub in shortening until it is as fine as coarse corn meal.

3. Add enough sour milk to make a stiff dough.

4. Turn onto a floured board. Knead slightly.

5. Roll into a rectangle ¼ inch thick. Spread with soft butter. Sprinkle with sugar and cinnamon.

6. Roll as for jelly roll. Cut in slices ¾ inch thick. Spread an additional tablespoon butter in the bottom of the pan and sprinkle liberally with sugar. Add a few pecans, if desired.

7. Place rolls, cut side down, on sugar mixture. Bake in hot oven. Turn out of pan immediately. Serve sugared side up.

8. Brown sugar may be used in place of white sugar to make butterscotch rolls.

Amount: 12 buns   Temperature: 475° F.   Time: 15-20 minutes
<u>See page 24</u>

INDIVIDUAL SHORT CAKES

2 cups all-purpose flour
½ teaspoon Arm & Hammer or Cow Brand Baking Soda
½ teaspoon salt
⅓ cup shortening
¾ cup sour milk or buttermilk (about)
Butter
Strawberries, crushed and sweetened

1. Sift, then measure flour. Sift again with the baking soda and salt.

2. Cut or rub in shortening until it is as fine as coarse corn meal.

3. Add enough sour milk to make a stiff dough. Turn onto a floured board. Knead slightly.

4. Roll ¼ inch thick. Cut with 3-inch floured biscuit cutter.

5. Place half of biscuits on ungreased baking sheet. Brush with melted butter. Place remaining biscuits on top to form a second layer. Again brush with melted butter. Bake in hot oven.

6. Break open and put fruit between and on top of layers. Garnish with whipped cream if desired.

Amount: 6 servings   Temperature: 475° F.   Time: 15 minutes

QUICK ROLLS

2 cups all-purpose flour
½ teaspoon Arm & Hammer or Cow Brand Baking Soda
½ teaspoon salt
2 tablespoons shortening
¾ cup sour milk or buttermilk (about)
Melted butter

1. Sift, then measure flour. Sift again with the baking soda and salt.

2. Cut or rub in shortening until it is as fine as coarse corn meal.

3. Add enough milk to make a stiff dough. Turn onto a floured board. Knead for 2 or 3 minutes.

4. Roll ¼ inch thick. Cut with 2-inch cutter, well floured. Fold in half, pressing edges firmly together.

5. Place slightly apart on a greased pan. Brush with melted butter, cover and let stand 20 minutes in a warm place.

6. Bake in hot oven 10 minutes, then brush again with melted butter and complete baking 10 to 15 minutes. Brush with melted butter once more. Serve immediately.

Amount: 12 rolls   Temperature: 475° F.   Time: 20-25 minutes
See page 24

LEMON CLOVER ROLLS

2 cups all-purpose flour
¾ teaspoon Arm & Hammer or Cow Brand Baking Soda
½ teaspoon salt
¼ cup sugar
⅓ cup shortening
½ cup sweet milk
3 tablespoons lemon juice

1. Sift, then measure flour. Sift again with the baking soda, salt and sugar.

2. Cut or rub in shortening until it is as fine as coarse corn meal.

3. Add the combined milk and lemon juice, stirring quickly to form a soft dough.

4. Turn onto a lightly floured board. Knead slightly.

5. Form dough into balls about the size of marbles. Place 3 balls in each muffin tin. Sprinkle with sugar. Bake in hot oven.

Amount: 12 rolls   Temperature: 450° F.   Time: 20 minutes

APPLE DUMPLING

2 cups all-purpose flour
½ teaspoon Arm & Hammer or Cow Brand Baking Soda

½ teaspoon salt
⅓ cup shortening
¾ cup sour milk or buttermilk (about)
1½ cups diced apples
Sugar and cinnamon
Butter

1. Sift, then measure flour. Sift again with the baking soda and salt.

2. Cut or rub in shortening until it is as fine as coarse corn meal.

3. Add enough sour milk to make a stiff dough.

4. Turn onto floured board. Knead slightly.

5. Roll into a rectangle about 20 inches long and 10 inches wide. Cut into eight 5-inch squares.

6. Place a small amount of apple in the center of each square. Sprinkle lightly with sugar and cinnamon. Dot generously with butter. Fold corners of square toward the center and join them over the apples. Place in greased baking pan. Bake in hot oven 15 minutes.

7. Then pour over them a syrup of 1 cup sugar and ½ cup water that has been heated until all sugar is dissolved. Return to oven and bake 15 minutes longer. Serve hot with Hard Sauce.

Amount: 8 dumplings   Temperature: 425° F.   Time: 30 minutes
<u>See page 24</u>

CREAM SCONES

2 cups all-purpose flour
½ teaspoon Arm & Hammer or Cow Brand Baking Soda
¾ teaspoon salt
2 tablespoons sugar
4 tablespoons shortening

Grated rind of 1 orange (optional)
¾ cup sweet thin cream or top milk
4 teaspoons vinegar
1 egg

1. Sift, then measure flour. Sift again with the baking soda, salt and sugar.

2. Cut or rub in shortening until it is as fine as coarse corn meal. Add orange rind.

3. Combine cream and vinegar. Add to flour mixture, stirring quickly to form a stiff dough. White vinegar makes a whiter product.

4. Turn onto floured board. Knead slightly. Roll ⅜ inch thick. With a sharp knife, cut in diamond shapes. These may be cut in half lengthwise if desired. Brush thickly with slightly beaten egg.

5. Place on ungreased baking sheet. Bake in hot oven.

Amount: 12 scones   Temperature: 475° F.   Time: 10-12 minutes

HAM ROLLS

2 cups all-purpose flour
½ teaspoon Arm & Hammer or Cow Brand Baking Soda
½ teaspoon salt
⅓ cup shortening
¾ cup sour milk or buttermilk (about)
1½ cups boiled ham, ground
¼ teaspoon dry mustard
Butter

1. Sift, then measure the flour. Sift again with the baking soda and salt.

2. Cut or rub in the shortening until it is as fine as coarse corn meal.

3. Add enough sour milk, stirring quickly, to make a soft dough.

4. Then turn onto a floured board. Knead slightly.

5. Roll into a rectangle 10 inches by 6 inches. Spread with soft butter, then with the ground ham which has been mixed with the mustard.

6. Fold the dough into three layers, folding the long sides toward each other. Flatten slightly with rolling pin by rolling lengthwise. Cut with a sharp knife into strips 1 inch wide.

7. Stand rolls about ½ inch apart on baking sheet. Bake in hot oven.

Amount: 12 rolls   Temperature: 475° F.   Time: 15-20 minutes

Muffins

WHOLE WHEAT MUFFINS

2 cups whole wheat flour
1 teaspoon Arm & Hammer or Cow Brand Baking Soda
½ teaspoon salt
4 tablespoons sugar
½ cup raisins
1 egg, well beaten
1½ cups sour milk or buttermilk
3 tablespoons shortening

1. Combine flour, baking soda, salt, sugar and raisins. Mix well.

2. Combine well beaten egg, milk and melted shortening.

3. Add the liquid ingredients to the dry ingredients, stirring only until dry ingredients are dampened.

4. Fill greased muffin tins ⅔ full. Bake in hot oven.

Amount: 12 muffins   Temperature: 425° F.   Time: 20-25 minutes

BREAKFAST MUFFINS

2 cups pastry flour
½ teaspoon Arm & Hammer or Cow Brand Baking Soda
½ teaspoon salt
2 tablespoons sugar
1 cup sour milk or buttermilk
1 egg
4 tablespoons shortening

1. Sift, then measure flour. Sift again with the baking soda, salt and sugar.

2. Combine milk, well beaten egg and melted shortening.

3. Add liquid ingredients to dry ingredients. Stir only until all the dry ingredients are dampened.

4. Fill greased muffin tins ⅔ full. Bake in hot oven.

Amount: 12 muffins   Temperature: 425° F.   Time: 20-25 minutes
<u>See page 33</u>

OLD FASHIONED CORN BREAD

1 cup all-purpose flour
¾ teaspoon Arm & Hammer or Cow Brand Baking Soda
1 teaspoon salt
1½ cups corn meal
2 eggs
1½ cups buttermilk or sour milk
3 tablespoons shortening

1. Sift, then measure the flour. Sift again with the baking soda, salt and corn meal.

2. Combine well beaten eggs, buttermilk and melted shortening.

3. Add the liquid ingredients to the dry ingredients, stirring only until smooth.

4. Turn into a well greased pan. Bake in hot oven.

Amount: 8 x 8 inch pan   Temperature: 425° F.   Time: 25-30 minutes

APPLE FRITTERS

2 cups flour
¾ teaspoon Arm & Hammer or Cow Brand Baking Soda
½ teaspoon salt
2 tablespoons sugar
¼ teaspoon nutmeg
2 eggs
1⅓ cups sour milk
2 tablespoons shortening
2 cups diced apples

1. Sift, then measure the flour. Sift again with the baking soda, salt, sugar and nutmeg.

2. Combine well beaten eggs, milk and melted shortening.

3. Turn the wet ingredients into the dry ingredients. Beat until smooth. Fold in apples last.

4. Drop by spoonfuls into deep fat and cook to a rich brown, turning frequently. The fat when ready for frying fritters should be 375° F., or it should brown a cube of bread in 60 seconds.

5. Serve hot with syrup.

Amount: 8 servings

ORANGE RAISIN MUFFINS

2 cups all-purpose flour

¾ teaspoon Arm & Hammer or Cow Brand Baking Soda
½ teaspoon salt
⅓ cup sugar
½ cup raisins
1 egg
⅓ cup orange juice
½ teaspoons grated orange rind
⅔ cup sour milk or buttermilk
⅓ cup shortening

1. Sift, then measure the flour. Sift twice with the baking soda, salt and sugar. Then add raisins.

2. Combine well beaten egg, orange juice, rind, sour milk and melted shortening.

3. Turn the wet ingredients into the dry ingredients. Mix only until dry ingredients are dampened.

4. Fill greased muffin tins ⅔ full. Bake in hot oven.

5. For variation, ¾ cup orange juice can be used in this recipe in place of a combination of orange juice and sour milk.

Amount: 12 muffins   Temperature: 425° F.   Time: 25 minutes

GRIDDLE CAKES · WAFFLES

SOUR MILK GRIDDLE CAKES

2 cups all-purpose flour
1 teaspoon Arm & Hammer or Cow Brand Baking Soda
1 teaspoon salt
1 tablespoon sugar
2¼ cups sour milk or buttermilk
1 egg
1 tablespoon shortening

1. Sift, then measure flour. Sift again with the baking soda, salt and sugar.

2. Combine well beaten egg, milk and melted shortening.

3. Add the liquid ingredients to the dry ingredients, stirring only until smooth.

4. Heat griddle slowly and evenly. To test the temperature of griddle, place a few drops of cold water on it. If the water forms bubbles which dance merrily, the griddle is the correct temperature for baking the cakes. Grease the griddle, using an unsalted fat, unless it is the type of griddle which requires no greasing.

5. Pour batter from tip of large spoon on griddle. The spoon should be of a size to hold sufficient batter for one cake.

6. Bake, turning each cake when it is browned on the underside, and puffed and slightly set on top. Turn only once. Serve immediately on warm plate.

7. For Flapjacks, make large sized cakes, sprinkle generously with grated maple sugar, then stack 4 or 5 deep and serve in wedge shaped sections.

Amount: 2 dozen cakes   See page 33

WAFFLES

2 cups all-purpose flour
1 teaspoon Arm & Hammer or Cow Brand Baking Soda
½ teaspoon salt
1 tablespoon sugar
2 egg yolks
2 cups sour milk or buttermilk
¼ cup melted shortening
2 egg whites

1. Sift, then measure flour. Sift again with the baking soda, salt and sugar.

2. To the well beaten egg yolks, add the sour milk and melted shortening.

3. Add the dry ingredients gradually to the liquid, beating in well.

4. Fold in the stiffly beaten egg whites.

5. Bake on hot waffle iron.

Amount: 6 four-section waffles   See page 33

Helpful Kitchen Hints

DRIED BEANS AND PEAS. When parboiling dried beans for baking, the addition of ½ teaspoon of baking soda to each 2 cups soaked beans makes the beans tender in a shorter time. When baked, the beans have a much sweeter flavor than those parboiled in plain water. All dried legumes such as lima, soy, kidney or navy beans, and peas, have a better flavor if treated in this manner.

SCALLOPED DISHES. Scalloped potatoes or other scalloped dishes are sometimes spoiled in appearance by curdling of the milk. ¼ teaspoon baking soda to each pint of milk prevents the curdling.

HOMINY. In the preparation of hominy, use 1 ounce of baking soda (2 level tablespoons) and 3 pints of water to each pound of field corn. Dissolve baking soda and add corn. Bring corn to boiling point, cover and simmer 1½ hours. Hulls and black eyes can be removed by rubbing between the hands. 6 or 7 washings will remove all traces of soda.

SPINACH. When washing spinach, add a small amount of baking soda (about ¼ teaspoon for each peck of spinach) to the last rinse water. Cook as usual. The vegetable will retain its lovely fresh color.

RHUBARB AND GOOSEBERRIES. When stewing rhubarb or gooseberries, add ⅛ teaspoon baking soda for each 2 cups. This reduces the quantity of sugar required by ⅓. For each 2 cups of rhubarb or gooseberries, use ⅔ cup sugar in place of the usual cup.

PEACHES AND APRICOTS. To skin peaches and apricots quickly and easily, blanch in a baking soda solution. To blanch, make a solution of ½ cup baking soda to 2 gallons of water. Bring to boiling point and while actively boiling, immerse fruit (using a wire basket) until skin is loosened. Remove fruit, wash at once in clear cold water and remove skins by rubbing.

BAKED HAM AND PORK CHOPS. When baking ham or pork chops in milk, the addition of ¼ teaspoon baking soda to each pint of milk prevents the curdling which so often detracts from the appetizing appearance of the meat.

CORNED BEEF. When boiling corned beef, add ¼ teaspoon baking soda for each pound of beef. This will improve the color and flavor of the meat. Cabbage and other vegetables can be cooked in the same water without becoming dark or slimy.

CLEANING MEAT. Clean all meat as soon as unwrapped with a baking soda solution (1 teaspoon baking soda to 2 cups water). This removes foreign matter and dried blood. Put on a clean plate and place in refrigerator.

FOWL. After drawing fowl, wash well, both inside and out, with a baking soda solution (1 tablespoon to 2 quarts of water). Let solution run through the bird several times. Rinse well with clear water. Pat dry with clean towel.

FISH. Clean fish, both inside and out, in a baking soda solution (1 tablespoon to 2 quarts of water). Dip entire fish in the solution; wash quickly and rinse in clear water. Dry immediately and store in cold place. Before opening, wash clams and oysters with a brush dipped in the baking soda solution. Fresh shrimp and other shell fish should be washed well in the same strength baking soda solution before cooking.

CREAM OF TOMATO SOUP. To prevent curdling, when preparing cream of tomato soup from canned or home-made tomato purée, add ⅛ teaspoon baking soda to each cup of soup or purée before adding it to the milk.

Baking Soda Cleans—Too

TILE FLOORS AND WALLS. To cleanse such surfaces soiled by splashed water, etc., sprinkle baking soda on a damp cloth and rub briskly. Wipe with cloth wrung from clean water and dry. The surface will be clean and shiny. Arm & Hammer or Cow Brand Baking Soda will not harm tile or any composition material resembling it.

ASH TRAYS. Unless cleaned daily these receptacles become offensive. To cleanse, scrub trays either with a baking soda solution (a small handful to a quart of warm water) or use a damp cloth sprinkled with bicarbonate of soda. Rinse and dry. Brass and copper trays may require polishing with a woolen or other polishing cloth.

LINOLEUM OR CONGOLEUM. Dissolve a large handful of baking soda in warm mop water and clean. Rinse with clean water. Do not allow water to seep under floor covering. This method of cleaning leaves the linoleum (inlaid or printed) bright and clean and it will be neither sticky nor slippery.

WASH-BOWLS, TUBS, ETC. Hard water is often responsible for scum and sediment; grease and dirt adhere to surfaces. To remove these sprinkle with baking soda and rub briskly with a damp cloth. Baking soda is immediately soluble and will not clog drains or injure the finest porcelain or enamel.

DRAIN BOARDS. Dampen surfaces, whether wood or enamel, and sprinkle with Arm & Hammer or Cow Brand Baking Soda. Rub with a damp cloth, rinse and wipe dry. Rubber or other composition drain boards may be cleaned in the same way. Bicarbonate of soda, while being a most effective cleanser, will not harm any of these surfaces.

GAS AND OIL STOVE BURNERS. Make a solution of one-quarter pound of baking soda to one gallon of hot water. Bring to a boil. Immerse the burners and boil for one hour. They will operate like new.

ENAMELED SURFACES. Enameled table tops, stoves, washing machines, etc., may be cleaned either by sprinkling the soda on the dampened surface or washing with a baking soda solution (a handful to a basin of warm water). This removes the oil or grease film which holds the dirt, and leaves the surface clean and odorless.

MILK BOTTLES. Pour a little baking soda into the bottle, half fill with cool water and shake. If milk is dried on, let bottle soak for a few minutes. Cold water removes milk more quickly than hot, as hot water causes a coating of milk to adhere to the glass. Bicarbonate of soda not only hastens the cleansing process, but sweetens the bottle. Milk cans, pails and all milk containers are cleansed in the same manner, using more baking soda in greater quantities of water.

FIRE EXTINGUISHER. Arm & Hammer or Cow Brand Baking Soda is unsurpassed as a fire extinguisher. It not only smothers the fire, but generates carbonic acid gas which temporarily envelopes the flames, shuts off the air supply or oxygen, and so extinguishes the fire.

BREAD BOXES. Cake and bread boxes, cooky jars, etc., after washing with soap and water, should frequently be well rinsed with a baking soda solution, a handful of baking soda to one quart of water. Rinse in clean water and dry thoroughly. This treatment keeps them fresh and free from odors.

CASSEROLES. Food that is burned onto or adheres to casseroles is easily removed by soaking for a few minutes in warm water to which a small handful of baking soda has been added. The bicarbonate of soda loosens the encrusted particles.

REFRIGERATORS. Baking soda, refined mild bicarbonate of soda, is a soluble cleanser, sweetener and polisher, and cannot scratch the smoothest surface. It will remove odors by breaking up the oily surface films, prevent fermentation by removing mold and retard the growth of bacteria, thus keeping the refrigerator sanitary and fresh.

Whether the refrigerator is electric, gas, oil or ice, keep the inside sweet and clean by wiping all surfaces with a soft cloth wrung from cool or lukewarm water containing a handful of baking soda to each quart of water, or by generously sprinkling baking soda on a damp cloth and briskly rubbing the surface to be cleaned.

Keep ice cubes free from stale or musty flavors by cleaning the ice trays each week with baking soda in a similar fashion. Also with a baking soda solution, wash the food containers and the chilling tray beneath the freezing unit.

In ice refrigerators, periodically remove drain pipe, ice chamber, pan, trap and flues for a thorough washing with a hot solution of water and baking soda. Rinse with clear water.

A baking soda solution (a small handful to a basin of water) may be used to wipe the outer surfaces when soiled.

SILVER CLEANING. Silver may be cleaned easily and thoroughly by placing it in an aluminum pan filled with a hot solution of baking soda, salt and sugar, or in an enamel or granite pan, using a similar solution and a small piece of aluminum such as a measuring spoon or pot cover. Use about a tablespoon of each, baking soda, salt and sugar, for every quart of hot water. Select a large container for convenience. Place the silver in such a way that it is completely immersed and that each piece comes in contact with the aluminum or a piece of silver touching the aluminum. Let it stand until tarnish is removed and the silver becomes shiny and bright. Heat if necessary. Rinse in hot water and rub dry. This method removes absolutely no silver, hence it prolongs the life of silverware. Since the aluminum article will be blackened in the process, do not use one you care about keeping bright.

Large pieces of silver, such as candlesticks, cake plates, pitchers, etc., may also be cleaned this way, making sure they are completely immersed in the solution.

CUT GLASS. Goblets, tumblers and other cut glassware are satisfactorily cleaned by rubbing the surface with a paste made of Arm & Hammer or Cow Brand Baking Soda and water. Rinse with cold water and rub with a soft brush. Soap is unnecessary.

CHOCOLATE POTS OR MIXING BOWLS. Dried-on chocolate needs a little coaxing for removal. Sprinkle with baking soda, fill dishes with warm water and let soak until their turn comes in the washing.

ODORS. Odors from dishes in which fish or onions are cooked, are quickly killed by sprinkling baking soda in the dish and wiping out thoroughly with tissue paper. Then wash in hot soapy water, rinse with hot water and dry.

DOG KENNELS AND FEEDING DISHES. Scrub the inside of dog kennels frequently with a baking soda solution, one package to three gallons of hot water. Rinse.

To promote the health of pets, their feeding dishes must be cleansed frequently. Let soak in a baking soda solution (a handful in a pan of warm water). This loosens dried-on food. Wash and rinse.

BEVERAGE SERVICE. Cups, coasters, pitchers, glasses, spoons, punch bowls, fruit containers, etc., are all successfully cleaned and sweetened with bicarbonate of soda. The baking soda is best applied by sprinkling on a moist cloth and then gently rubbing the object until clean. Rinse with warm clear water and dry with clean towels having no lint.

To clean bottles, decanters, flasks, shakers, etc., which do not permit interior cleaning by hand, pour the baking soda into the container and add a little warm (not hot) water. Shake well until clean, then rinse with fresh water and allow to drain. This leaves the containers in a sweet clean condition. Repeat after each use.

Cocktail sets made of glass, silver, etc., are excellently cleaned by these methods.

THERMOS BOTTLES AND JUGS. To keep thermos bottles and jugs clean and sweet, put a handful of baking soda in jug or bottle, partly fill with warm water and shake well. Rinse with clean water. Corks and other closures used for the bottles and jugs are kept odorless by rubbing with moist baking soda.

VEGETABLE COOKERY

To PRESERVE the fresh green color of beans, peas and greens, a pinch of baking soda (a pinch is less than ⅛ teaspoon) should be added to the cooking water. Red vegetables will be most pleasing in appearance if a little vinegar is added to the cooking water.

A little vinegar in the cooking water will keep white vegetables from yellowing. In the case of old carrots, a pinch of baking soda will shorten the cooking time.

TIME TABLE FOR VEGETABLES

Vegetable	Boiled	Steamed	Baked
Asparagus	15-25	30-40	
Beans, cut	25-30	40-45	
Beets, whole	35-40		
Brussels Sprouts	10-15	15	
Cabbage, chopped	15-20		

Time: Minutes

cut	20-25		
Carrots,			
whole young	15-25	20-30	
whole old	30-40	40-50	
Cauliflower, wh.	15-20		
flowerets	8-10	15-20	
Onions, small	20-25		60
Peas	20-30	30-40	
Potatoes, white	30-40	35-50	45-60
Potatoes, sweet	25-30	30-40	45-60
Pumpkin, cut	30-40	40-50	60
Spinach	10-15		
Squash	15-20	30-35	40-60
Turnips	30-60		

TABLE OF WEIGHTS AND MEASURES

3 teaspoons	1 tablespoon
4 tablespoons	¼ cup
5⅓ tablespoons	⅓ cup
8 tablespoons	½ cup
12 tablespoons	¾ cup
16 tablespoons	1 cup or ½ pint
A dash	less than ⅛ teaspoon
2 cups	1 pint
4 cups	2 pints or 1 quart
4 cups flour	1 pound
2¼ cups granulated sugar	1 pound
2 cups brown sugar, firmly packed	1 pound
3½ cups confectioners sugar	1 pound
2 tablespoons butter	1 ounce
2 cups butter	1 pound

1 medium egg	2 ounces
8-10 egg whites	1 cup
14 egg yolks	1 cup
Juice of 1 medium lemon	3 tablespoons
½ pound nutmeats	1 cup nutmeats, chopped

TEMPERATURE AND TIME TABLE

Slow Oven 250° F.-325° F.	Moderate Oven 350° F.-375° F.	Hot Oven 400° F.-500° F.	Time
		Biscuits	15 minutes
		Muffins	25-30 minutes
	Cookies	Cookies	8-15 minutes
	Layer Cake		25-30 minutes
	Loaf Cake		45 minutes
	Loaf Cake (thick)		50-60 minutes
Fruit Cake			3 to 4 hours
Sponge Cake			1 hour

LITHO IN U.S.A.   F-500-1-38

www.ingramcontent.com/pod-product-compliance
Lightning Source LLC
Chambersburg PA
CBHW081127080526
44587CB00021B/3777